Everyone's a Genius & We're All Approaching Infinity

by Sal Fratto and Ben Underhill

Everyone's a Genius & We're All Approaching Infinity
FIRST EDITION, Paperback
ISBN 978-0-692-70417-2

10 9 8 7 6 5 4 3 2 1

Cover Art: Copyright © 2015 Rachel Miller
Cover and Book Design by Benjamin Underhill

Published through createspace.com
Book title font from www.jennasuedesign.com
Email questions to BenUnderhillBooks@gmail.com

Everyone's a Genius &
We're All Approaching Infinity

Dedicated to Mr. Foti, who taught us AP US History, and many long-lasting life lessons.

Thank you Foti.

"There is not a particle of life which does not bear poetry within it."

-Gustave Flaubert

Poetry and Prose

The unknown origin of words is an integral part of why I wake up every morning; not to discover the answer, but to question more and more. Ben and I have both been composing poetry on our own, and in the middle of one night, full of delirium and a lack of sleep, we decided to collaborate on our first poem together. The intent of this book is to emit our individual emotions, combine our feelings, and provide a bridge from your world to each of ours, and to the one we have created, together.

My eclectic tastes in music and poetry combine with my metaphysical thoughts to develop words that I wish to help people. I want to help, even if it is only one person, feel that they can simply 'feel.' Growing up, I'm pretty unsure of anything, and poetry, music, and art are like a blanket over my body during a winter storm. Writing poetry gives me a sense of security, being in love gives me a sense of liberation, and creating gives me a sense of immortality- nothing ever dies. I hope someone finds this, long after I am gone, in a dusty attic, and reads it to their children. I, we, truly hope you enjoy this combination of words sewn together by Ben and myself, and I hope we make you feel that you can feel.

-Sal Fratto (S.F.)

Poetry is a significant part of life, whether we realize it or not. Sal and I did realize this, and we created this idea early in the dawn of one day with the intention of spreading inspiration through poetry. It is not meant to be read necessarily, but rather it is meant to be felt. You see, art, literature, music- these are the expressions of the mind. But poetry- poetry is the expression of the heart and soul. It is one of the many physical manifestations of human emotion that surrounds us. It is a four-thirty-in-the-morning text message. It is the teardrops falling from your best friend's eyes (whether he or she is happy or sad, or both, is up to you to decide). It is the emotion you feel when you experience art.

Part of my family motto is "vivite et amate semper," which roughly translates from Latin to "live and love always." This is my wish to you: live every day as if it were the best one of your life. Live while sharing your light (it will not take away from the amount of light you have, only brighten the world). Love what you love without regret. Love passionately because "people may not remember what you say or do, but they will remember how you made them feel" (a paraphrase of Maya Angelou's quotation). Maybe further down the road of your life, you will pick this book up once again, and remember the emotions you felt once upon your life.

-Ben Underhill (B.U.)

3 AM on the First Night

Art is the reason humans live
Art is the muffled sound of you giggling between my sheets
Art is the indecipherable imprint of your lips
Along the frame of my spine
Only to me...

Art is the tear-stained paper of a last photograph
Art is the racing heartbeat
During our first kiss
Art is the beauty of nature's destructive and creative forces
Only to me...

Art is packing bags
Art is not wanting to leave
Art is hundreds of miles of distance,
Yet sleeping right next to you
Art is trying to find you
In every shape of every cloud
Art is perspective
Art is falling off
Art is clinging on

Art is a daytime sunset
Art is a nighttime sunrise
Art is the stars in your eyes
Art is the envy the sun has
Of your entrancing smile
Art is the way you smile
When you sing the song of your soul
Art is the tranquility of when I'm with you
Art is my mind thinking of the world's full potential

Hey, I think I see your lips
Hey, I think you're on my mind

-S.F. & B.U.

Everything Had Been Spinning

Everything had been spinning
For as long as I can remember
Inside of the mind
Outside of the net
Lying on our backs
Loving the distance
Hating how far away we are
The top
The edge
The escape
I don't want to leave
The sky winks at you every
Single
Night
Another breakthrough
Break through
The figurative, imaginative
Barriers
We don't exist
We are the creators of what exists
Everything
Nothing

We're in the palms of each other's hands

Are running up and down my thigh

One night

Cry

I want to go back there

Someplace familiar

Somewhere I've known that I know that I don't know

Anywhere

Else

But my mind

Forever exasperated by the cruel,

Incandescent speculations

Eccentricity

Entropy

Soothing

Eye

Cannot unfeel you

-S.F.

What it Was

I read her eyes
Like a new loved novel
Her warmth changing me
From stressed
To obsessed

I'm a mess
The lights in our minds flicker
I remember
Every contour and freckle
Or joy in her real smiles

I remember the way the stars
Formed to make her eyes
I feel insane
Love
Destroying me time and time
Again
Again
Again

The others were sirens

But she's an angel

With coffee stained teeth

And messy hair

Reminding me

Not of who I used to be

But of who I can become

She reminds me

Of what it's like to be wanted

To be kept around

Because my company is enjoyed

Please don't let it be a dream

-B.U.

The Prettiest Girl in the Room

The prettiest girl in the room

Whispers

Fragments of sentences

Are all of my dissolutions

Imagined

Space

Between

You and me

Venus

Mercury

Space

The prettiest girl in the room

Long dark hair

Black stains along the inside of my

Chest throb(s) and

Ache(s) painlessly

Breathing the air

Between the leftover space of our fingers

Intertwined...

Suffocation.

How does one recognize such beauty?

Coinciding

Inhabitants of the same

Zone

Out of my mind

In yours

In your eyes

The sky does not exist, for you are the highest

The lightest

Half-conscious alleviation

Respiration

Inside of you

Inside of me

Breathing until

Limitations

Have sent me running to you

-S.F.

The Birth of One, the Life of Two

In this world
I wandered lonely
For nearly a few decades.
Love was sometimes found,
But always lost,
And it was not what I thought.
For each time it was lust
And heartbreaks
And every damned "goodnight, I love you"
That I wasted on her.

I had given up on love,
And then I met a new her,
And my world lit up
In a way I had never seen.
As the music drowned out
All the passing cars
As we drift down the freeway,
She sat shotgun
With the wind in her hair.
Our hands intertwined at our destination,
And our lungs were tired

From shouting our favorite songs.
At the end of the night,
We departed,
And I said "goodnight, I love you,"
And she said it back,
And meant it.

-B.U.

Saxophones

I can stare into my neighbors' houses
And take in their channels
I can hear saxophones in the clouds
I can see myself being struck down by anxiety
And I can see you running and laughing around
In a circle
I'm living in a circle
Ready or not
There you go
Hundreds of miles of worry and fear
And television programs I don't get on my server over here
Don't watch anyone else.

-S.F.

16

Photograph Copyright © Benjamin Underhill

For My Friend S.M.

Misunderstood, yet still loved
Feeling alone feels like darkness
Creeping into her mind
But the color and beauty of her soul
Keep her mind free and creating
She thinks she's broken
But a mosaic is made from broken glass
And is still art
Like her.

She rests her head
Thinking she'll never find the right guy
While a thousand miles away
A guy dreams of a girl like her
The world between them
The sweat on her brow
She makes her friends proud
While she screams inside
She's an angel without wings
But she'll make his heart fly.

-B.U.

Photograph Copyright © Rhea Rifflard

The Bowery

I love you more than the stars love the night sky
More than socks love my frostbitten toes
More than delirium loves all of the junkies set aside in the
Bowery
More than blankets love the straight standing hair
On our bodies
While they're intertwined with each other's
And the moon
Is watching me watch you
And the movie doesn't end
It simply cycles

-S.F.

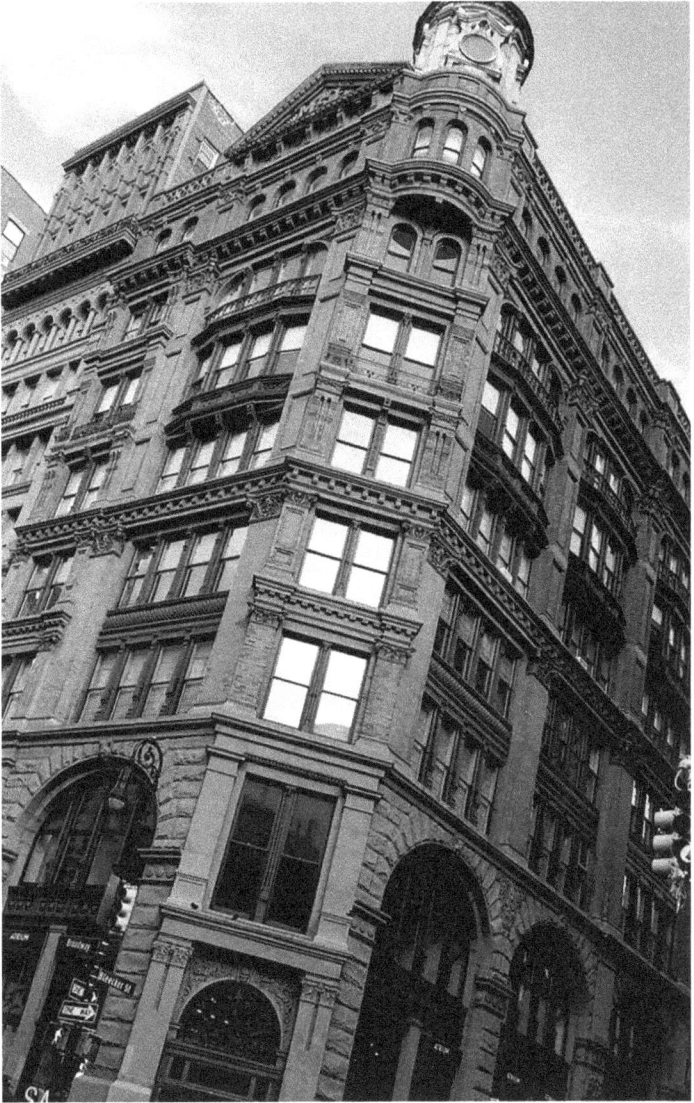

The World's Cycle

In destruction, there is creation
In creation, there is light
In light, there is hope
In hope, there is inspiration
In inspiration, there are blanks
In blanks, there is emptiness
In emptiness, there is possibility
In possibility, there is innovation
In innovation, there is advancement
In advancement, there is replacement
In replacement, there is destruction
In destruction, there is creation

-B.U.

Photograph Copyright © Benjamin Underhill

Can You Tell That I Worry Too Much?

Can you tell that I worry too much?
Can you tell that I'm insane?
Can you tell that I'm in love with you?
Can you tell that I'm telling you everything?
One by one
Step by step
Never skipping
Unless it's arm in arm with you
I feel my happiest feelings
Like a child
On the swings
I swear I can pump my legs
...I just want a push

-S.F.

Photograph Copyright © Shannon Moran

What is Existing?

What is existing, if not a dream
Where everything is not always bliss?
How we breathe and speak and learn destroys us
Unless we are coexisting
Together
We can achieve greatness
But others are cursed to wish harm and failure
While the unanswered questions
Pound in our heads
We want the answers to questions
We don't understand
Questions like
What is existing?

-B.U.

Photograph Copyright © Lena Diaz

Passing Between a Million Dimensions

I'm staring at you in the sky
You look at me, too
Through the trees
Misty fog
Let's make full circles
After dark,
After ours (hours)
Streetlights blaring
Blinding
Twice as bright
I don't mind you
On the weekdays
How long does it take?
One revolution?
What is resolution...if your presence discards all problems?

-S.F.

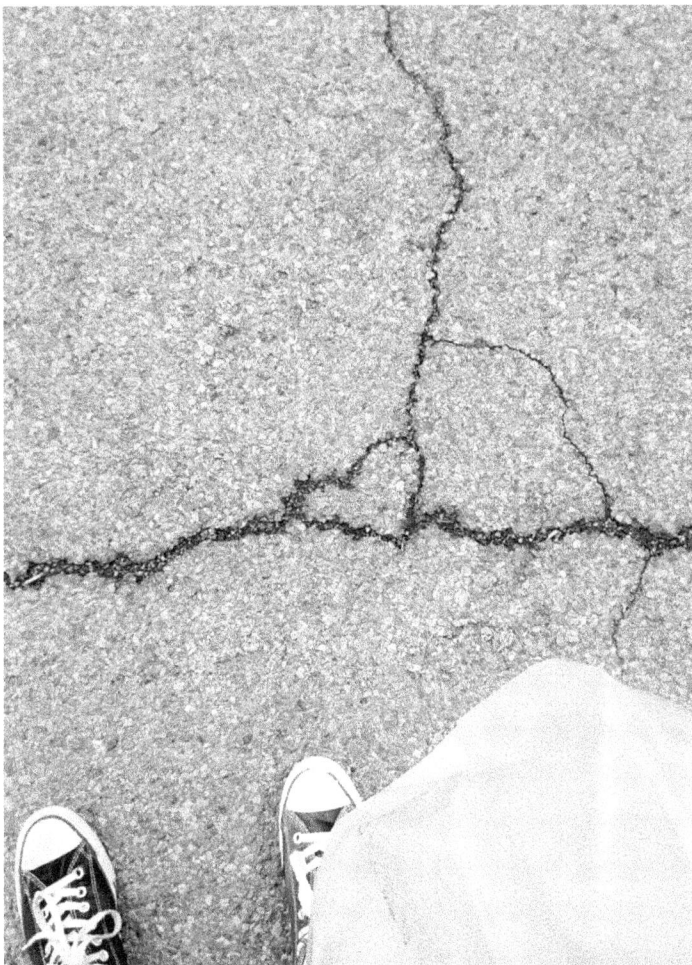

Photograph Copyright © Salvatore Fratto

For My Friend B.M.

Her face lights up with hope
A beauty a lucky few possess
Her eyes sparkle like stars
Forming a constellation of awe

The joy she radiates
Makes the world around her light up
I don't know if she's a goddess or an angel
But she is more than what she thinks she is

She is more than the scars
She is more than the pain
She is more than the feeling of not being good enough
She is a poem to the world

-B.U.

Photograph Copyright © Rhea Rifflard

I Can Hear You Smile

I think you fell asleep
I think it was next to me
Fidgeting
Every position
Every decision
Every acquisition
I hear pianos in my head
I hear violins
I hear gorgeous
Emulations
No one
Never
The fog is dawning
As night wraps its arms around morning
Mine have never left their spot
On your body
On your mark
Get set...
Stay.

-S.F.

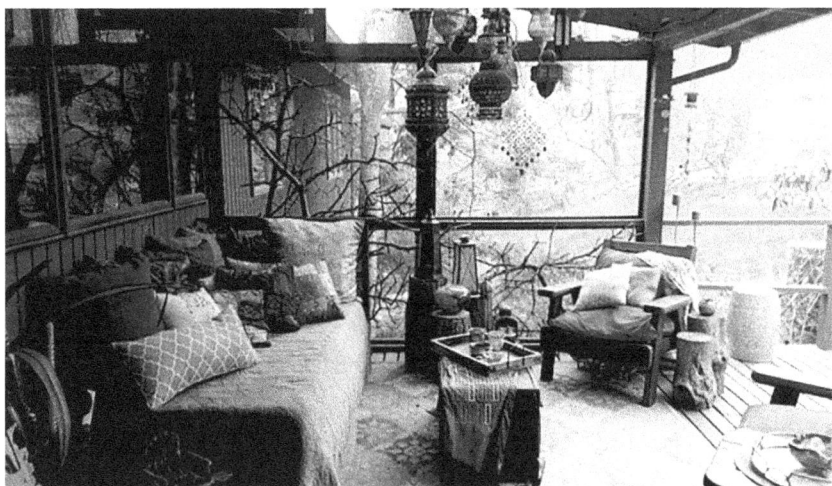
Photograph Copyright © Rhea Rifflard

Part I: So This is Love

So this is love:
An uncontrollable desire
To be with you,
To be us.
Maybe it's just our auras connecting,
But I feel my stomach
Erupting with butterflies
At the simple sight of you,
Reminding me of every love song
I've ever heard.
All of this while
Your voice lulls me to sleep
In the darkest of times.
And if I could pluck one star
From the sky for every reason I love you,
Well then, darling,
I'd hold the universe
In the palm of my hand.

-B.U.

Photograph Copyright © Benjamin Underhill

<u>I Love it</u>

I love the way you dance
Even when you're standing still
I love the way you sing while being silent
I love the way you cry without tears
The way you dream with your eyes open
The way you do every little thing

-S.F.

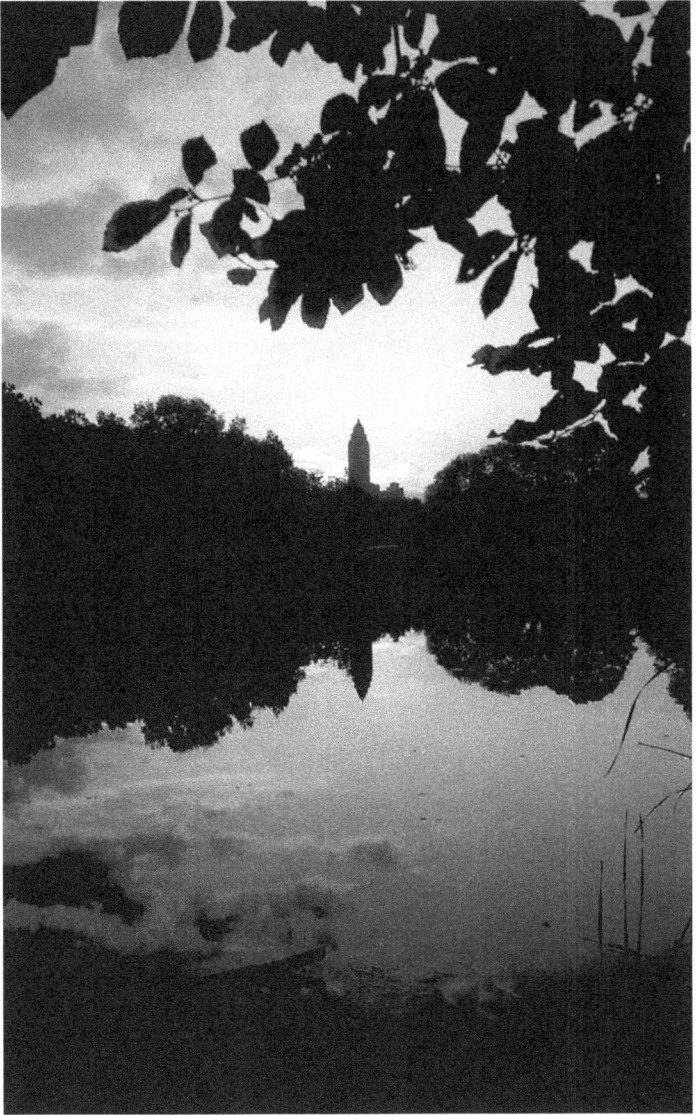

Photograph Copyright © Justice McCray

Part II: So This is Suffering

So this is suffering:
A simple goodbye,
A simple no more.
You seem to remind me
Of my darkest fear.
It was, and is, and still will be
That you would wake up one morning
And no longer love me,
Love us.
Do you remember that day
I burned my tongue on my coffee,
And you said I should heat it up more?
"Do you even care?" I asked.
You said I knew the answer,
But I swear I didn't, and I still don't know.
Timidity courses through my veins and arteries.
I shudder when your name appears
On my phone at 3 AM with three little words.
You know what they were.

-B.U.

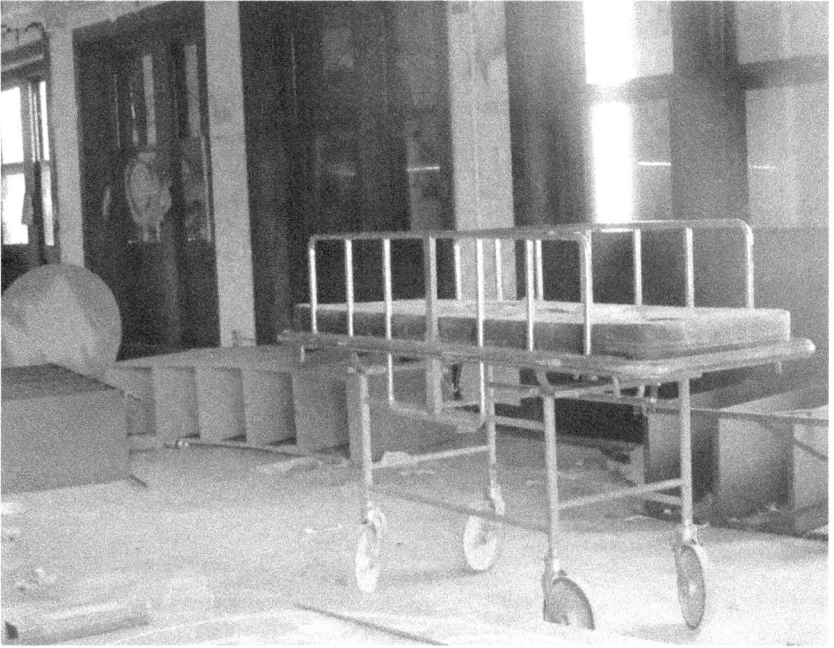

Photograph Copyright © Rhea Rifflard

Trampolines

I like not knowing

I like looking up

I like the sky

I like seeing myself with you

Inside

Nonexistence

Devastates me

Trampolines

Square fascinations of the universe in full

Split in two

In me and you

In you and me

Dampened

A universe of infinite combinations

Inside a universe of infinite combinations

Inside a universe of infinite combinations...

-S.F.

Photograph Copyright © Salvatore Fratto

Part III: So This is Moving On

So this is moving on:
A bittersweet release of breath, and feelings,
And countless memories.
Maybe the memories I'll hold on to,
But crop them to make them pretty.
You deserve that at least.
Perhaps moving on is best for me,
Even though I know I won't be able to
For months.
The light in my eyes is gone,
But the fire in my heart burns
Hotter than ever before,
And hopefully
I won't get burned
The way I did
Staring into your eyes,
Brushing against your skin,
Pressing my lips against yours.
Letting go is like a scar,
It will fade, but will remain.

-B.U.

Photograph Copyright © Benjamin Underhill

Dashes

I've been waiting a long time

To open you up

Tear down all of the fucking walls

Eyes closed

Eyes opened

Capability

You may have thought you may have

You may have

Up and down and up and -

Weeeeee

Bumps in the road

Crash right into the bricks

Float away

Take a swim. . .

You and I are like an ocean

We all have ripples

But don't you think...?

It's fun to ride the waves,

Together?

-S.F.

Photograph Copyright © Shannon Moran

<u>Maybe</u>

Maybe it's the way she smiles
Or the way her laugh brightens the world
Or maybe it's the way her embrace
Thaws my frozen heart
Maybe it's the way her passion shines
Maybe it's just me

Maybe it's the way she talks
Or the way her words feel like music
Or maybe it's the way her eyes
Remind me of oceans
Maybe it's the way she loves the world
Maybe it's just me

Maybe it's the way she moves
Or the way her joy spreads
Or maybe it's the way her tears
Should only be from happiness
Maybe it's how she looks at art the way I look at her
Maybe it's just me

-B.U.

Photograph Copyright © Brianna Matteo

Petunia

Emasculate me with your body

If you want to

Waiting on the edge

Breathing slowly

Petunia, oh Petunia

Emasculate me

Show me your face again

Kissing it like I used to

I see the Freedom Tower!

It's falling off

The face

Of the Earth

Compares to the sunrise over my little house

In the middle of everything, I can still see you

-S.F.

Photograph Copyright © Rhea Rifflard

In the Now

The second day of school
Still shows the chaos of order.
Everyone is thinking of the future
And not thinking in the now.
It is a side effect of time,
Always rushing about to be on time,
And not living in the now.
There used to be a time
When we, as humans,
Lived "in the now."
We saw the world
Day by day,
Not second by second.
We carry out our lives
In the future,
Always planning,
Always surviving,
But rarely living
In the now.

-B.U.

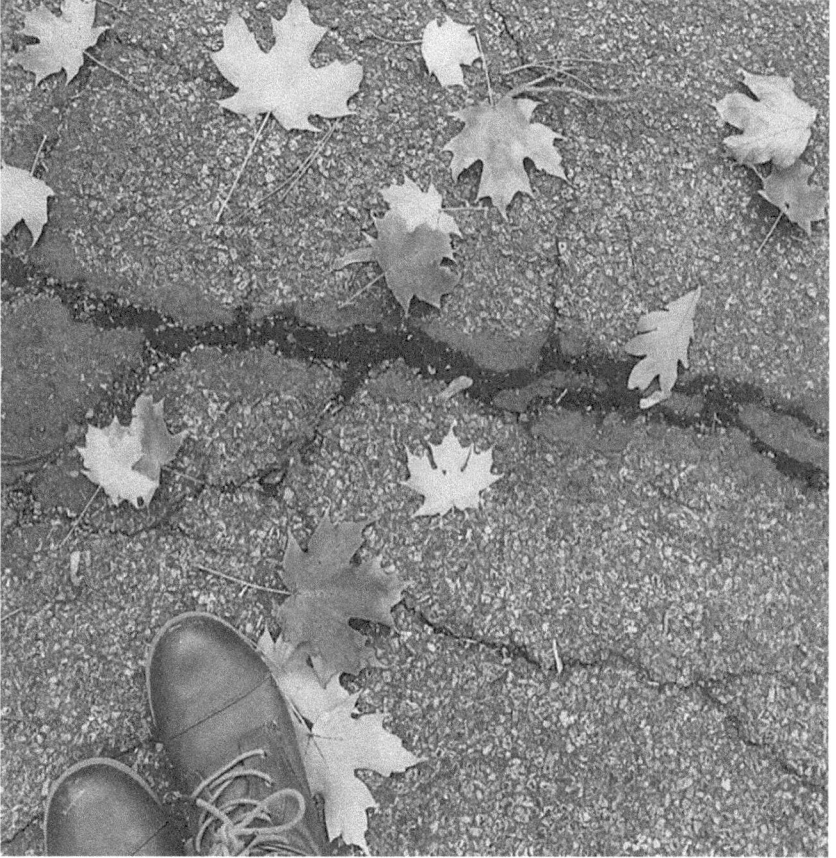

Photograph Copyright © Olivia Fava

Snow Day

Don't you want to take a walk

In the snow?

It seems so long

Your hand in mine as we make our way across the bridge

That never ceases to sway.

Your body

Hello,

Dive in

The oceans can hear me

Whispering

Waving

Bye-bye

-S.F.

Photograph Copyright © Benjamin Underhill

Broken Pieces

Shards scatter on the floor
As my heart shatters like a plate
Yes, the broken pieces
Can be glued back together
But there will always be little pieces
That can't be found
So empty cracks are left behind
Where it was once filled and pure
And again the plate will crack
And again and again and again
And each repair
Will leave that plate (my heart)
Missing broken pieces

-B.U.

Photograph Copyright © Joseph Alberts

Your Eyes Are Red in the Big Blue Ocean

Maybe we were shot
The night rolled into tomorrow
I was thrown a million years back
A million miles forward
You and I have lived
Before time
And will remain
Much long after it
Holding hands through the oceans
The eight wonders
You are the first
And last
Incisive
Undocumented
Unprecedented
Press me into the wall
Lately I've been feeling as if I've felt you
Since the world first opened up its eyes
I've opened up mine
I don't mind the tingling
I don't mind the burning
Swimming pools
Chlorine

Explore

Please don't deplore

Me

Hey Sweetheart,

Your eyes are red

Why don't you come over here?

I can try

I can try

I can die

Every night

Let's feel

Better

-S.F

Another Late Night

I do this to myself
Almost regularly:
I stay up late,
And before you know it,
I'm awake again
After only a brief night's sleep.
I burn myself out,
Staying awake
Terrified
That I would lose you in a dream,
Or wake up from the one
You are.
You are
A dream.
The best I've ever had.
I am scared,
Scared of the unknown
In the raging ocean
That is me
And my thoughts.
Yet somehow,
For some reason,
You stay.

You calm the sea

And you dim the light

In order to save its fuel.

You crush the walls I put up

And put a flamethrower

To my heart

To thaw it out.

You add to the incomprehensible emotions

That rush through me

At speeds that would make a bullet

Shocked.

Yet these emotions

Are stirred to perfection,

And they shimmer,

Just like the universes in your eyes.

I feel calm,

Just by the thought of you,

And it amazes me.

You are here.

I am here.

And we are together.

-B.U.

Transitions

I will die when you do
Everything you've ever done
With a disregard to all real expectations
Much appreciation for resting with you
In my bed
I'm too free spirited to make it in the real world

-S.F.

Photograph Copyright © Kayla Holterman

To My Best Friend's Future Boyfriend

You've won her heart
And you may be the lucky first
But the adventure has only begun
You'll learn her past
Present
And hopeful future
Along with the location
Of every freckle and scar
On her body

The simple questions
Like her favorite song
Should be followed
With the eternal question
Of why
Why one song makes her happy
And another makes her cry
And why concerts are her second home

Learn the way she likes her coffee
And surprise her with it
And don't be afraid to make her smile

I am still learning about her
Things you may learn
In a sleepy phone call
Mumbled into the phone
So value every word she says
And be damn sure to value her
With every breath you take

Love her eyes and smile
And the way her hands fit into yours
But most of all
Keep the smile in her eyes alive
And the fire in her heart kindled
There's only one of her in this world
And thank God she exists

Remember this
And cherish her
Please

-B.U.

Something Will Become of Us

Something will become of us

Long, long, long deep beneath Boston piers

Feel a new

England

Impermeable constellations

Winks from the sky

Tell me that I'm alright

Three headed airplanes

Helllloooo

Helllloooo

And I pray for nothing more than for them to abduct me

Subduction

Can you drown in the fire?

Drown in eyes

I's...

I feel myself floating out of my body into another

I feel myself losing my mind

I feel like I'm alive

I feel like I'm dying

You can't drown

Life

Preserved

I whisper to you

That I can picture a picture inside of your body

Every movement,

A sculpture

Every word,

A painting

Every breath,

A sketch

I want to be your drawing pad

Float with me

Hahahaha

Yes,

Float with me

The outer lining of your complexion melts into the layers

Lay her down

Lay me down

Discoveries

Overlapping

In my lap

Our words

Garlic remnants

You can taste it on my breath

Remember the intonation

Keep speaking

Tie

Tie

Tie

A knot

Will not

Keep us afraid

Keep me feeling like I feel something

One

Two

Three

Forever

Can you feel yourself feeling as if you're alive?

Deceased

The chill

The heat

The passing between a million dimensions all at once

Balance

Peace

How can you make me feel like this?

How can two individuals become a superpower?

How!

How!

How!

-S.F.

Photograph Copyright © Kayla Holterman

<u>You Said "Forever"</u>

My feelings conflict
And your eyes burn my soul
I can't shake these emotions
That leave me barely conscious
It kills me
That she used to kiss me like a prince
But now her lips feel like poison
I sit here shaking
Remembering my haunted past
The words you burned into my mind
And the long nights we spent together
When you said, "Forever"

-B.U.

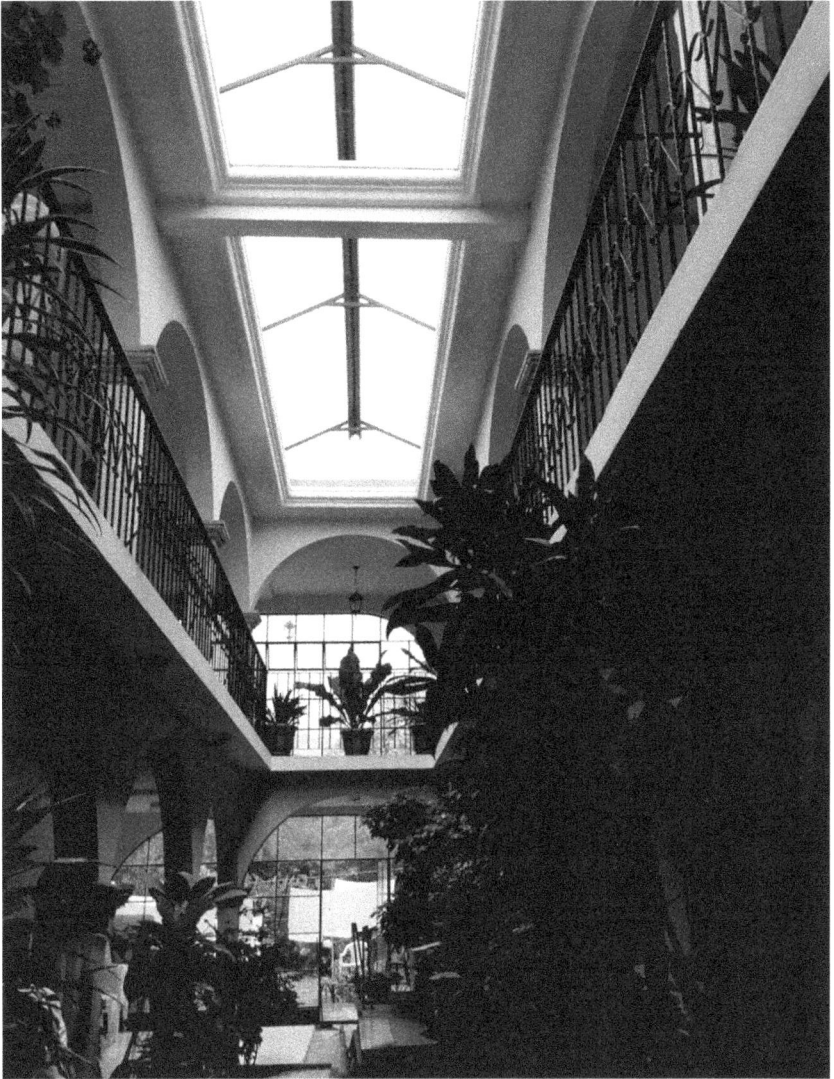

Photograph Copyright © Benjamin Underhill

Pulses

Darkness embraces me
Over
Analytical hearts
Erase me
Skin
Warm, so warm
Skin
Against mine
Pressure
Released
Atmospheric bodies dissolve
Into the
Evergreen...

-S.F.

Photograph Copyright © Justice McCray

Past Nights

The poisons of life
Come in twos:
Cigarette smoke
And the taste of you.
But if there's anything
That remains true,
It's that with everything
We've been through,
I cry out still,
The stage lights blue,
Begging on repeat, and forgetting
Everything I knew.
I realize now
That the only thing to do
Was try to escape,
But the place I always ran to
Was you.

-B.U.

Photograph Copyright © Lena Diaz

Fish Kisses

Music whispers in my ear
Your lips touch your lips touch my lips
Touch my lips
With fish kisses
Glisten
Listen to the music
That echoes in the sky
At night
When you cry
I cry
When you die
I die
I could do this millions of times
I really like the feeling of anticipation
We make
Love
You've got an open mind
You can take a swim in mine
For a little while
Everything's okay
I've learned to grow with the flowers
Water me
I want to feel like I feel when I'm lying on your chest

Tell me the truth

Do you want me

Just as much as I want you?

Look into my eyes

A streak

A rainbow

I see green

Blue

Purple clouds

I see a world that is spinning

I see a world that is tilted

The opposite direction

I want to ride

Any combination of sounds squeezed through you

Make me shiver

Make me shake

Close your eyes

See your face

Pressed up against mine

I think it's time

Rise

Rise

-S.F.

Past Nights (Reprise or Relapse, I Don't Remember Which)

Heroin and your lips
Are the things that I hate most;
One kills you,
While the other destroys me.
I said it once, and I'll say it again.
Under candlelit stars
And the off-white moon,
The thoughts still haunt me
With every overdose I take:
The thoughts of you.
My arms and lips and lungs
Burn with the rest of my body.
Our body,
Our connection,
Is lying face down
In the Hudson River
Because you pushed it off the bridge
To meet its reflection
Below.

-B.U.

Photograph Copyright © Benjamin Underhill

<u>Fall Up</u>

Right between the eyes

Metacarpal

Tunnel

Run run run

Fall

Fall   Up

Up

Up

Infatuation to the rising simulation

My bones

Resting

Your bones

That cast a moonlight so bright

The sky holds

Earth

Is layered

Stare into yourself

Staring into the stars

Am I the only one,

Or the only one evaporated?

-S.F.

Photograph Copyright © Rhea Rifflard

Through the Seasons

Look, look
Do you see me there alone?
Missing your touch and voice
Passing the autumn months' fun

Hush, hush
Do you hear me call to you?
Begging for you back
Living the winter months' sadness

Feel, feel
Do you understand my touch?
Burning with new passion
Feeling the spring months' renewal

Look, look
Do you see I've moved on?
Laughing with new people
Enjoying the summer months' freedom

-B.U.

Photograph Copyright © Rhea Rifflard

Peekaboo

I've read the book a few times
And suddenly a thousand
Over lapping
Underneath you
Underneath me
If you were to look at me
From the sky,
Would you stay up high
Or jump without a parachute?
It got dark as we went up here
Coming back down does not exist
Where the hell am I?
Approaching the clouds
What keeps the moon from falling?
You can almost see the curve of the sky
Tonight I'll melt into my cushions
Melt into the constellations
Our feet dangling off the edge of the mountain
Of the Little Dipper
Dip her
Spin her
Make her lose control
She'll make you lose the mind

You never thought you had

I never think

I think

I think

I know I love you

Laughter,

Peekaboo

-S.F.

My City Dream

Have we ever considered
A simple, stupid date
To anywhere at all
To my mind or to your soul
Perhaps the city
Is where people like us belong
That way
We don't run out of adventures
Or stories to tell each other
Or maybe we need it
To hide in the crowd
And make our own realities
In our daydreams

-B.U.

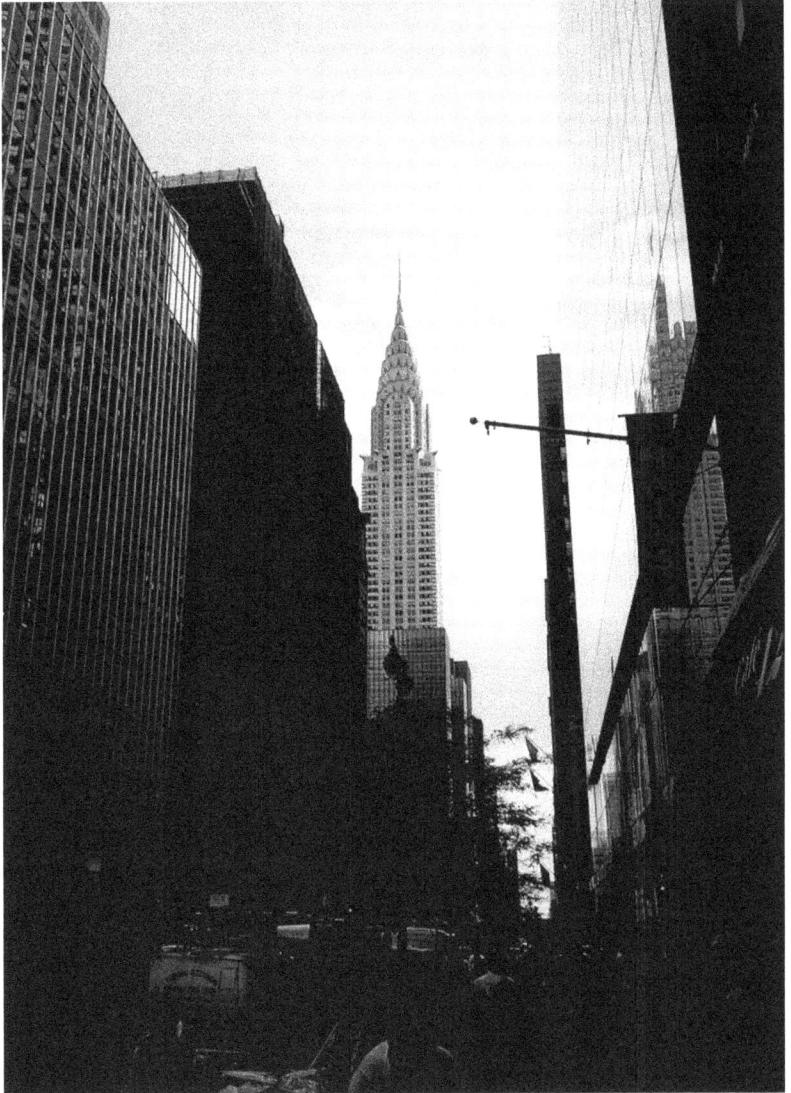

Photograph Copyright © Justice McCray

Can You Hear Me, Darling?

Hush, can you hear me Darling?

You, me, floating to the bottom of the sea.

Gloomy, gaiety, lingering, comprising ripples

Whispers

Screaming

Grasp your palm

Ascension

Gasping,

Breathing

Breathe with me

Slip through the never

Ending

Qualm

Quiver

To be satisfied is to be

Lying...

Dissolving

Through a mattress

See into your mind

And

Under your clothes

Perhaps it's alright

It's all right

Just a drip

A whole storm

We'll clear away

Is this it?

For I've only dipped my feet in...

-S.F.

Complexion

The human race has been seeking
An answer to a question
We don't even know
Proving that
As a species
The more we learn
The less we understand
I don't understand, but listen
I love the sound of thunder as I rest
Because I know it can't hurt me
Unlike the sound of your voice
And every little thing
You used to whisper
Into my neck

-B.U.

Photograph Copyright © Benjamin Underhill

Mine; Mind

My mind is numb
I cannot breathe
She reminds me of who I used to be
The world distorts
I don't know what's real
I hate forgetting what it's like to feel
Tickled by unexpected doses of her jaw line
It takes more muscles to smile
Exercise
Every single night
One behind the other
All alone
In my head
I go crazy every time I close my eyes
Three
Penetrate the soul
With aspiration
Exasperation
As someone else
Pushes you
Right between the thighs
I don't think I'm alive

Regret

Fear

We used to have it all, but now we have nothing

The course of human existence

Led us to each other

But now it leads us away

-S.F.

Poetry

Poetry begins as a simple feeling
Not even a thought
And then quickly
It turns to a simple complexity
Or a complex simplicity
A way to make people
Feel
Because feeling
Is a human's biggest fear
We repress emotions
Ignore ourselves
All because
We refuse to believe
Bad things happen
To good people
And that sometimes
The good guys
Lose
Feelings scare us
And sometimes rightfully so
Because bad feelings exist
And poetry is evidence of this
But poetry can give us a feeling

Of hope

Of life

Of all the wild emotions we face

Day after day

Throughout our terrifying dream

That is life itself

At the base of the pyramid

At the root of it all

Is poetry

-B.U.

Being a Human Being

Why must I

Stay trapped inside

Worlds

No one knows

Except for me

Except for you

I heard shotguns

Our bodies

Curled up

Between time

Wring me out

And tell me twice

About what it feels like for you

Full of houses

Full of noises

I hear screaming

From the top floor

Break me down

Build me up

I long to be the tingling

Racing up and down your thigh

I dream to be the thoughts you think as you sleep

I aspire to be every little thing you've wanted in a human

Being

A

Human

Being

Is

All

We've

Ever

Needed

Please

Forgive

...me.

-S.F.

City Lights (Were, Maybe, Not)

City lights in her eyes
The sorrow escaping
Replaced by joy
Laughing
Crying
I miss seeing her so happy
I miss seeing her
I miss her
With city lights in her eyes
But when she mistook lust for love
Is when she began to ruin me
And I tried to bring it back again
But further I drowned
Sinking
In a sea of her
Or what I thought was us
Perhaps we
Were
Maybe
Not

-B.U.

Photograph Copyright © Brianna Colón

Maybe it's the Way You Flow

Maybe it's the way you flow

In and out

Never leave my side

I want you to run around the world

I can imagine

Galaxies

Overlapping and intertwining

Your legs over mine

The warmest yet most freezing

Clime

My heart races

As if we're just

Unsure of how

Could we ever

Fall in love

Into me

I promise you

Don't lie

Alone

Empty beds

Lonely

Incomplete

I don't want to find either of us

Caught between someone else

They

No single

Breathes

Touches

Feels

Talks

Reciprocates

That it's okay to feel

Inside of you

I feel

Inside of you

How long have I been sleeping?

Ouch,

While the idea

Stings much worse

Than anything can

Inside of our heads

I know this

Is

Real

-S.F.

Misunderstood

Sunlight
Starlight
Do you understand my fight?
My pain
My gain
The days when it rains
She was alcohol
She was menthol
That 3AM phone call
A reminder of what I lack
Begging for me back
As thoughts emerge from the black
Of my mind

-B.U.

Photograph Copyright © Rhea Rifflard

Percolations

We'll spend most nights crying, wishing it was day

Most days dreaming, wishing it was easy,

When the sun goes down;

Nothing is real

No one is breathing

I want to know what scares you most

Mendacious

Facetious

If I told myself I won't make it

Define

Affluence

A collection of whispers and essence

Lingering through the basement

I'm so worried about being trapped in

Hahaha

As if I let myself

Fly by

My eyes

Your eyes

Liberate my appreciation

-S.F.

Photograph Copyright © Sabrina Toto

Music

Music pulses through our bodies
A feeling new and old
The rhythm and melody
Working together
Like celestial bodies

We feel the open road ahead
Driving down I-95
Letting it lead us everywhere
And nowhere
Only to the stars
Only to each other

Maybe the music is her
And I'm listening
To every breath
And word
And late night thought

-B.U.

Photograph Copyright © Benjamin Underhill

Shoot Us

Maximum levels
Comfortable stability
Molds my ever
Needing
Sedation
Of a cerebrum
I'm not sure I've got one
Two
Three of the same thing
Every day
Sets of
One phrase
Couple more
Words
Relieve tensions
Sweet
Heart
Slow dancing to autonomous
Deep voices
Shoot us
From the wall
Shoot us
We're together

Shoot

No one else

Knows

May

I

In

August?

Put you to sleep

States

Estates

Fluffy fluffy water bed

Fluffy fluffy

Reaching for you

Reaching for me

Hold me

Holding you

Under the stars

Ceilings often resonate

Time continuum

Spaces between

You & me

I love you

-S.F.

Our Spark

We all have a spark of light

Though some may be dim

Guiding us in the dark

Until we are free again

When our dreams are filled with hope

A dying star before it goes supernova

We are nova

We are new

There is beauty in death

And the things that result

From it

But none more so than life

And the rebirth of it

The rebirth of me

Hoping, dreaming

Pretending to not exist

We exist

Forever

If we are written

And remembered

-B.U.

Photograph Copyright © Rhea Rifflard

Everyone Has Love for Everyone Somewhere

Sometimes I miss people
I've never met before
Sometimes the pink sky
Makes me cry
Sometimes I hear voices
In the back of my head
Sometimes, I want to die
I can wrap you up
In my arms
Is the only place I'd like to be
One star in a constellation
I'd like to be the one you look at
I'd like to think of something better to say
Than goodbye

-S.F.

Photograph Copyright © Sabrina Toto

Take Me Along

This is a love song

Or a ballad

Or a cry for help.

In reality, I'm not sure

What this is,

Or what we are.

But I do know

That you're on my mind

Day and night.

Soon we will part

For months at a time,

But will you remember me?

Or will it end

With a phone call on a rainy day?

In the grand scheme of things,

All of my metaphors to stars

And sunsets

And music

Will never compare

To you

-B.U

Photograph Copyright © Olivia Fava

We Will Make it

Please
Please tell me that this is going to last forever
That every single time
That we are underneath my bed sheets,
You're home

I don't understand
Yet I do
I understand that we're burning
Combining
Opening our souls and filling them with each other

Love me fully
Excluding all fear
Knowing this is real
Yet petrified
Of life to come
But I promise you
That if you keep your eyes closed
And your heart open
You can build a world
And I can be your partner

We can change our worlds

Breaking walls and building love

If we sit

And listen

We hear the sound of the heartbeats

Breaking and in love

Are we geniuses?

Will we reach infinity?

We approach it

And live it

-S.F. & B.U.

Acknowledgements from Sal

I send my warmest gratitude to:

Mr. Foti, for teaching us that there is more to life than what is presented to us, and to look past the surface

E.E. Cummings, for breathing through a hard cover book placed beside my bed

Elizabeth Fischer, for keeping my feet on the ground and my head in the clouds

Zachary Siper, for making folk-punk with me

My band mates in Elephant Jake: Colin Harrison and Reinier Potgieter, for existing

Joey Alberts, for riding trains and swimming in a stranger's pools with me

My mother, for always supporting me no matter what. Love, lots and lots of it

My father, for giving me the 'Satisfaction' that is Rock and Roll. Yes, that is a Rolling Stones reference

All of my lovely Minisink friends, you know who you are

Ben Underhill, for texting me in the middle of the night with a desire to combine words and emotion to make people happy

Acknowledgements from Ben

I would personally like to thank:

Mr. Foti, for being an incredible teacher and mentor, a passer of wisdom from his generation to ours

Josh Stewart, for being a devoted pastor and role model

Terry Sandler, for teaching me in ways I am still discovering, but most importantly for breaking me out of my shell and into the spotlight

Emily Evans, for keeping me on track with my life's journey, and existing in general

Shannon Moran, Brianna Matteo, Lena Diaz, and many others, for being the best friends a guy could ask for

My parents and brother, for their never ending love, care, and support, for which I can never be thankful enough

Jackson Galati and Mike Pirillo, for being amazing friends and encouraging me to be my best

All of my friends at Newburgh Free Academy, thank you for sticking with me through it all

Sal Fratto, for being a fantastic person, artistic partner, and most importantly, friend, and for responding to my text that one summer morning

"Every single soul is a poem."

-Michael Franti

www.ingramcontent.com/pod-product-compliance
Lightning Source LLC
Chambersburg PA
CBHW020914090426
42736CB00008B/628